# Maths all around us

# Size at school

Lisa Bruce

**Heinemann**
LIBRARY

Little Nippers

**www.heinemann.co.uk/library**
Visit our website to find out more information about **Heinemann Library** books.

To order:
☎ Phone 44 (0) 1865 888066
🖹 Send a fax to 44 (0) 1865 314091
💻 Visit the Heinemann Bookshop at www.heinemann.co.uk/library to browse our
catalogue and order online.

First published in Great Britain by Heinemann
Library, Halley Court, Jordan Hill, Oxford
OX2 8EJ, part of Harcourt Education.
Heinemann is a registered trademark of Harcourt
Education Ltd.

Editorial: Jilly Attwood and Claire Throp
Design: Jo Hinton-Malivoire and bigtop,
Bicester, UK
Models made by: Jo Brooker
Picture Research: Rosie Garai
Production: Séverine Ribierre

Originated by Dot Gradations
Printed and bound in China by South China
Printing Company

ISBN 0 431 17192 0 (hardback)
07 06 05 04 03
10 9 8 7 6 5 4 3 2 1

ISBN 0 431 17197 1 (paperback)
07 06 05 04 03
10 9 8 7 6 5 4 3 2 1

**British Library Cataloguing in Publication Data**
Bruce, Lisa
Size at School – (Maths all around us)
516.1'5
A full catalogue record for this book is available
from the British Library.

**Acknowledgements**
The Publishers would like to thank the following
for permission to reproduce photographs: Gareth
Boden.

Cover photograph reproduced with permission of
Tudor Photography.

The publishers would like to thank Annie Davy
for her assistance in the preparation of this book.

Every effort has been made to contact copyright
holders of any material reproduced in this book.
Any omissions will be rectified in subsequent
printings if notice is given to the publishers.

# Contents

# Size

This is Class One. They are finding out about size. Can you help them?

# Big and small

The **big** chair is for Mr Thompson.
The small chair is for teddy.

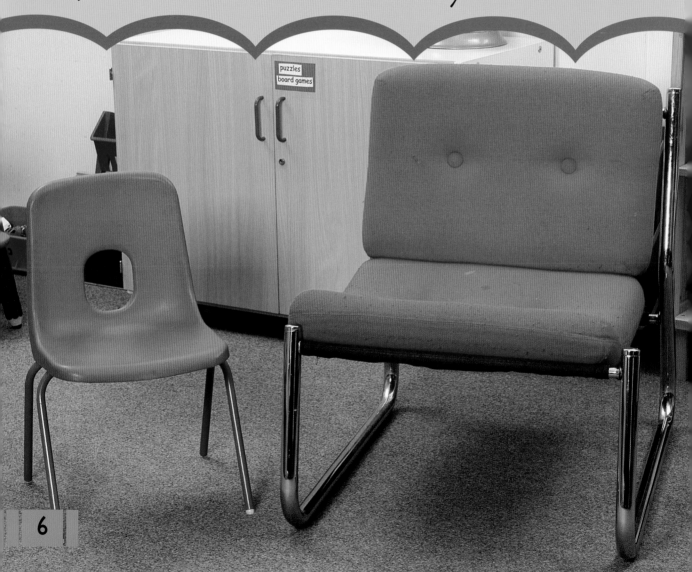

Mr Thompson is bigger than teddy.
Teddy is smaller than Mr Thompson.

# How **big** is your hand?

Splat!

These children are making handprints.

Put your hand over the handprint.
Is your hand **bigger** or smaller than
the handprint?

# Tall
## and
## short

Adam is being measured against a height chart. It shows him how tall he is.

# Tallest
## and
## shortest

Who is the
*tallest?*

Who is the
shortest?

# Long
## and short

Richard has short hair.

Louise has **long** hair.

# Longest
## and shortest

The green ruler is long.

The blue ruler is longer.

The yellow ruler is the longest.

The blue chalk is short.

The pink chalk is shorter.

The green chalk is the shortest.

# The same as

The children are lining up in the playground. The girls' line is the same length as the boys' line.

# What size?

Look inside the pencil case.

Which is the **biggest** rubber?

Which is the shortest ruler?

# All sorts of sizes

23

# Index

The end

## Notes for adults

*Maths all around us* introduces children to basic mathematical concepts. The four books will help to form the foundation for later work in science and mathematics. The following Early Learning Goals are relevant to this series:
• say and use number names in order in familiar contexts
• count reliably up to 10 everyday objects
• recognise numerals 1 to 9
• use language, such as 'more' or 'less', to compare two numbers
• talk about, recognise and recreate simple patterns
• use language, such as 'circle' or 'bigger', to describe the shape and size of solids and flat shapes.

The *Maths all around us* series explores shapes, counting, patterns and sizes using familiar environments and objects to show children that there is maths all around us. The series will encourage children to think more about the structure of different objects around them, and the relationships between them. It will also provide opportunities for discussing the importance of maths in a child's daily life. This series will encourage children to experience how different shapes feel, and to see how patterns can be made with shapes.

**Size at school** will help children extend their vocabulary, as they will hear new words such as *bigger, smaller, handprint, measured, height, chart, tallest, shortest, ruler, chalk, item, biggest* and *smallest*.

### Follow-up activities
• Make handprints, including adult handprints, and compare the sizes.
• Cut some ribbon into strips including some of the same length. Ask for the strips to be placed in order, longest first.
• Ask about animals that the children may know e.g. is a worm longer than a snake?
• You can also use size to help with positions. Ask the tallest child to stand behind the shortest one.